SELF CONFII
TEENAGE BOYS

How to Build, Improve, Boost, Restore and Strengthen Self-Esteem in Teen Boys

Green Smith

Copyrights©2021 Green Smith

All Rights Reserved

INTRODUCTON

CHAPTER ONE

WORKING ON HIS SELF CONFIDENCE

CHAPTER TWO

HOW TO MOTIVATE HIM

HOW TO HELP HIM

THE MOST EFFECTIVE METHOD TO HELP

ANOTHER METHOD TO HELP

CHAPTER THREE

RECOMMENDATION

CHAPTER FIVE

BUILDING CONFIDENCE IN YOUR TEEN BOY

CHANCES TO TRY NEW THINGS

CHAPTER SIX

WAYS TO IMPART ASSERTIVENESS SKILLS

BENEFIT FROM LEARNING TO BE ASSERTIVE

INTRODUCTON

Self-confidence is significant for everybody — particularly young people. Teenagers have the pressing factors of adolescence, friends and groundwork for this present reality burdening them consistently. You can help sustain and support your teen boy's confidence by supporting his inclinations, empowering correspondence and fostering his mental self-image.

Mother conversing with teenager child

1. Comprehend his qualities and shortcomings.

Having a fair of self-esteem includes knowing your own qualities while dealing with your shortcomings. Since an individual is sure about his qualities and gifts doesn't mean he must be presumptuous. Encourage your teen child to be glad for his capacities and gifts without being stooping to other people. A solid mental self-image can assist him with performing school, dominate in sports and relate with companions.

2. Put him in a good position.

Each individual is acceptable at something. It might take some experimentation, yet you need to help your high scholar discover his specialty. Whenever you have recognized his abilities, you can place your child in the situation to succeed. In case he's a talented competitor, permit him to play sports. The sound rivalry and kinship of group activities and coordinated sports can support confidence and fortify abilities. In case he's a capable performer, put resources into exercises or instruments if conceivable. Regardless of whether his qualities and loves aren't equivalent to yours, sustain his capacities and backing his decisions. Commendation his advance and praise his accomplishments, regardless of whether they're large or little.

3. Look at his friends

Friendships are essential to teenagers. The teen years are additionally when numerous children commit errors in regards to friendships. However you can't single out your child's friends, you can urge him to encircle himself with individuals who have similar qualities and character. Make your home where your adolescent can carry his friends to hang out. This will permit you to look at and screen his connections without being tyrannical. Show your teen that fellowships ought to be based on trustworthiness, regard and normal interest... not founded on what's cool or mainstream.

CHAPTER ONE
WORKING ON HIS SELF CONFIDENCE

End negative propensities so you don't give them to your kids. Don't generally put yourself down or be unfortunate of attempting new exercises. Bringing up sure youngsters can be restorative and can help you manage your own confidence issues. Do what you can to fortify your own mental self-image and lift fearlessness, while giving positive messages to your teen child.

Urge him to open up.

Speaking with child can be troublesome, and teen boys have a more troublesome time conversing with their folks about questions or issues than teen girls do. Urge your child to communicate his feelings, and don't debilitate him with old generalizations about masculinity ("young men don't cry"). You'll frequently discover young men are more able to open up when participating in an undertaking or movement, instead of simply plunking down for a discussion.

Attempt to connect with your ten boy in discussion during an action, for example, doing yard work, drawing or in any event, playing computer games. The absence of eye to eye connection might urge him to convey. When he begins talking with you about his issues or concerns, you'll have the option to work with him to discover arrangements and assist with building his confidence.

Give him greater duty.

Assist with boosting your teenager's fearlessness by showing your trust in him. By giving your child greater duty, you'll upgrade his self-esteem. Make it his duty to do the week after week yard work, go shopping for food or get more youthful kin from school. He can land his first position and pay his own phone bill or vehicle protection. Chipping in is another brilliant technique to help your teenager child have a positive outlook on himself. Rewarding others or working with a group to arrive at an objective will assist him with accomplishing a feeling of achievement and pride.

School is harder for young boys

Young boys are rasher and have a more troublesome time standing by and focusing than young girls do. In the interim, numerous schools aren't intended for brief breaks for the duration of the day that would help them — that would help all children, indeed. "So when young men can't sit and hang tight and the class is too large, what happens is they gotten problematic; they yell out the appropriate response," she says. "Furthermore, in light of the fact that they are disturbing, the way that they found the solution right and just couldn't clutch it and hang tight, doesn't check."

What checks is that they intruded, and when they're scrutinized more than once about it, it lessens their confidence. Not just that, "it likewise reduces their affection for scholastics and learning.

Bringing up that many school assignments can disgrace a boy, and that disgrace regularly goes to outrage. "And afterward everyone says, 'We have a particularly furious young man,' as though there's nothing to set off his resentment," he says. Then, at that point, if a kid can't read in kindergarten, "He says, 'I hate this. I hate reading.' What he implies is, 'I'm embarrassed that I can't peruse better."

CHAPTER TWO

HOW TO MOTIVATE HIM

Give Praise:

On the off chance that a boy is battling in school, instructors ought to make a special effort to search for freedoms to praise him when he accomplishes something right, regardless of whether it's a little thing. Not exclusively does a consistent deluge of recognition cause children to feel more joyful and more certain at school, yet clinicians say that "discovering kids being acceptable" can help emphatically shape their conduct, as well.

Challenge boys and permit them to develop abilities:

You throw boys as collectively into an extremely difficult circumstance, and let them sort it out and track down their own authority, "They'll return figuring, and 'We did it. We did it.' You'll see a huge load of certainty." Yet it doesn't need to get actually that limit. While teen boys might be behind teen girls, they can and ought to be relied upon to master abilities, directly down to making their own sandwich. "It includes causing a circumstance in which they can foster an ability and thus will have confidence.

Consistent contest

Boys are constrained into a severe pecking order in which they contrast themselves pitilessly with other boys. Boys are continually asking themselves 'Who's the tallest? Who's the quickest? Who's the greatest? Who's the head honcho?'" Dr. Steiner-Adair says. "Also, inside that come some genuine battles. What in case you're not? Imagine a scenario in which you're not athletic. I believe that is an immense weakness for boys

HOW TO HELP HIM

Talk about various, worse. Underscore the child's special characteristics, boys need to realize that we as a whole have various capacities and develop and learn at various rates.

Make your child media proficient.

Busman proposes sitting in front of the television with your kid or talking about the thing they're doing on the web. "Perhaps you see something on television that is depicting young men in stereotypic manner," she says. "Then, at that point you can say, 'Amazing, that is intriguing, not all young men are that way. Some young men are truly incredible at sports and some aren't.' And in the event that you see an especially decent good example, which is additionally a pleasant chance to get down on his credits: 'That person's so amazing. He's really smart, very much regarded by individuals around him, and he's benevolent.'"

More changed good examples.

Thompson noticed that displaying options in contrast to the athletic culture with male good examples – say, craftsmen, educators, gourmet specialists, artists – shows young men there are unique, genuine ways they can follow their gifts and still be esteemed. "Assuming you need to give young men certainty, then, at that point you give them the inclination that the abilities they have will win them the admiration of different men and boys."

Boys are relied upon to buck up

Indeed, even today, cultural standards frequently direct that young men should cry. "So what boys are instructed is the point at which you are tragic, when you are disturbed, don't get dismal however get frantic. We're gaining some headway, yet all around the circumstance is still to such an extent that by the age of 8, a kid needs to figure out how not to cry."

She noticed that we request this from young men exactly at the age where they're fostering the limit with respect to truly more profound, more significant feelings and sympathy to separate from their own bitterness and weakness." Later, these young men turned-young fellows need to figure out how to convey their considerations and feelings "without feeling that it's by one way or another an infringement of their masculinity.

THE MOST EFFECTIVE METHOD TO HELP

Allow them to cry.

You can let boys realize that they shouldn't be embarrassed about tears — you're not humiliated on the off chance that they cry — and that communicating sentiments doesn't mean they're frail.

Be open about sentiments:

Parents can likewise approve their boy's misery or outrage by urging them to discuss their feelings. Sleep time can be an incredible opportunity to check in with more young children, and with teens you can frequently get them to open up in the vehicle. "It doesn't need to be a profound discussion, simply assessing the situation, it's tied in with opening dialogue. Parents ought to likewise uphold their boy's feelings, disclosing to them that they're OK and that everybody has them. She adds that books can be useful in that office. For instance, she has one for her child called Troublemakers Have Sentiments, As well, with characters like a losing grappler and an achy to visit the family space explorer feeling pitiful. Books like this show young men that tragic or negative sentiments are typical and nothing to be humiliated of.

Demonstrating:

I would trust that we would likewise demonstrate a more solid perspective on being a kid who can communicate feelings, I figure the dad and different men in boy's lives can display being expressive about feelings and showing boys how they handle disappointments.

Teasing or tormenting:

Tormenting isn't solid for either the harasser or the person in question. At the point when you have a sexual orientation code that says there is just a spot for one at the extremely, top, then, at that point boys characterize themselves and improve themselves by pushing another person down, So we see a great deal of inconspicuous, and now and again not really unpretentious, parallel animosity and we see a ton of prodding." Any indication of shortcoming is reasonable game, including not being acceptable at sports or in any event, being excessively smart.

ANOTHER METHOD TO HELP

Support friendships and exercises with girls:

Playing with girls and associating with them in school and in co-ed exercises can eliminate intensity with other boys and allow young men an opportunity to foster interests that are not customarily manly with less fear of mocking.

Stress compassion:

Since early on, guardians can urge boys to know about how others think and believe, and consider those sentiments. A great deal of grade schools have a type of social passionate educational program, which show compromise, and she takes note of that it's useful for guardians to think about them so they can finish.

Try not to permit waste talk in your home:

Let boys realize that offending different children by calling them feeble or weaklings or failures (or more terrible) isn't adequate from them, or their companions, and ensure the grown-ups in your family don't do it, all things considered.

Adolescence is a critical time in the advancement of a boy's confidence. With rate of depression and uneasiness in boys proceeding to climb, it is significant that Parents know about how they can deal with assistance their boys foster self-confidence.

Make out time:

A crucial factor in a boy creating self-confidence is his feeling of having a place and acknowledgment at home. At the point when a boy feels acknowledged comfortable, it gives him an incredible springboard from which to move toward different aspects of his existence with certainty.

Having a place is imparted from various perspectives:

Notwithstanding, there could be no greater method to help your boy feel a solid feeling of having a place than investing energy with him. This can be doing ordinary things together, for example, consistently eating a feast as a family, unwinding before the television, driving in the vehicle, or doing schoolwork.

These add to his feeling of acknowledgment and having a place. Notwithstanding, assuming you need to supercharge a boy's feeling of connectedness and self-esteem, accomplish something with him that he appreciates, and do it routinely.

Words matter:

The words Parents use around their boy ought to be viewed as the fuel that takes care of his self-esteem.

A solid eating regimen comprising of confirming, aware and empowering words will assist with delivering a boy with a solid and positive perspective on himself. Notwithstanding, an eating routine of garbage words – disparaging names, affronts, consistent analysis and put downs – will create a boy who thinks that it's difficult to see his own value.

Sound words that are particularly significant for more youthful youngster young men's confidence include:

-Words that approve their sentiments, especially the negative ones

-Words that look for their assessment and welcome them to add to discussions.

Support, don't Praise: Utilizing positive words doesn't mean depending on useless commendation. Continually lauding boys, or disclosing to them they are exceptional or acceptable at something when they are not, makes similarly as numerous confidence issues as affronts and put downs.

Boys will in general know where they remain in the hierarchy. At the point when grown-ups attempt to tell boys something they instinctively know is false, the outcome is decreased self-esteem, as boys will feel felt sorry for or deceived.

CHAPTER THREE

RECOMMENDATION

My recommendation is to avoid commending your boy inside and out. All things being equal, center on empowering him. Applause centers on endorsement or examination with others. Nonetheless, consolation centers on certifying the sentiments, endeavors, character and development of the person. Consolation is connected to real recognizable practices and showed character qualities, and doesn't include utilizing modifiers, for example, "smart", "pleasant" or "exceptional".

The least demanding approach to urge your child is to affirm him when you see him show a beneficial characteristic. Recognize him when he settles on a decent decision, invests a genuine exertion, works on in a specific region, shows graciousness or persistence, exhibits boldness or genuineness, or takes care of an issue. You can likewise essentially offer thanks for him being him.

Take advantage of his natural abilities

Confidence is infectious. Extraordinary compared to other approaches to assist a kid with fostering a solid self-idea is to zero in on the everyday issues where he has a positive outlook on himself or presentations ability.

By reliably insisting your child's qualities, you help with building up his own conviction about what his identity is and what he is able to do. This conviction characterizes his self-idea, which he can't resist the urge to take into different pursuits throughout everyday life.

You will not assist a kid with working on his shortcomings by reducing his contribution in, or openness to, his qualities. In any case, by utilizing off those parts of life where he feels sure, you can help him increment his self-belief and ability in different regions.

CHAPTER FIVE

BUILDING CONFIDENCE IN YOUR TEEN BOY

Give Him Obligation

Your son's certainty will develop as he sees that you trust him to take on obligations in your home. He might protest and whine a piece, however having duties will assist him with seeing that he can do things and that you have sufficient trust in him to handover undertakings that you might have consistently done. Giving every day and week after week obligations will assist with setting him up for the future when he moves out and is all alone.

Pay attention to Him

Tell your son that what he needs to say is esteemed and significant. Give him a voice and truly pay attention to him. Have family committees where you examine family needs, objectives and choices and truly pay attention to the thoughts he brings to the conversation

Let Him Decide

It would be pleasant if we would enclose them by an air pocket and protect them in our home perpetually, however our boys should be allowed the opportunity to have an independent mind and even to commit errors to understand that the things they do have ramifications for themselves as well as other people. Your child's certainty will develop as he figures out how to use sound judgment in his life.

Discover Positive Good examples

As your son develops, assist him with discovering positive good examples to gaze upward to. On the off chance that our boys are not motivated by the right sorts of individuals, they will be roused by some unacceptable kinds of individuals. Individuals around them will impact their confidence and certainty.

Help Him Foster His Abilities

Assist your boy with fostering his abilities and interests. In the event that you see that he is looking into or that he is normally acceptable at something, let him realize that and urge him to learn however much he can. Likewise offer him chances to impart those gifts to other people.

CHANCES TO TRY NEW THINGS

Allow Him Opportunities to Attempt New Things and Even Fall flat. Disappointment is a gigantic piece of achievement. In the event that our children never figure out how to attempt new things and even to fall flat, they won't ever know the inclination that accompanies achievement. As Parents, it is truly hard to watch the hurt that accompanies disappointment, yet their certainty will develop as they push past the loss and prevail not too far off.

Show Great Cleanliness

As a previous secondary teacher, I can disclose to you that not all teen boys are shown appropriate cleanliness, and that can create some lovely foul circumstances.

I've encountered being in a room with the two limits — truly downright terrible scent or thereabouts much body shower that a haze of aroma chases after teenager boys. The manner in which an adolescent boy smells, will influence how he searches others.

With rec center class ordinarily being held right in the center of the school day, ensure you encourage your child to keep antiperspirant in his exercise center storage and to apply it every day during class.

Body spray is a reasonable option in contrast to cologne that is extraordinary for educating boys how to smell new the entire day, without trying too hard. Also, it is not difficult to apply. Help them to hold the can around 6 inches away and do one fast splash across their chest in a speedy 7 movement. That is it! No more haze of shower chasing after them!

Teen boys will have more certainty as they smell pleasant and look incredible!

Assisting my teenage son with growing a certain grown-up is vital to me. The teen years are hard and our teen children need direction, despite the fact that they would probably never let it out.

Children who appeared to be certain all through childhood might battle to keep up with confidence during the teenager years. For some, pre-adulthood is a period loaded up with self-question, a sketchy self-perception, and instability.

The uplifting news is, you can find ways to help your teen form confidence, which will profit your teenager in various manners. Boys who have certainty are more ready to deal with peer pressure, explore testing dating connections, use sound judgment, and recuperate from mishaps. Here are eight procedures that will ingrain deep rooted trust in your boy.

Advance Personal growth

Teenagers who battle to dominate an expertise might finish up they're finished disappointments. For example, a boys who experiences issues with math might choose they're not brilliant. Or then again a boy who neglects to make the soccer group might choose they'll never be acceptable at sports.

There is a good overall arrangement between self-acknowledgment and personal growth. Show your boy that it's feasible to acknowledge imperfections while additionally endeavoring to turn out to be better. Maybe than name themselves as "idiotic," help your teen see that while they're battling academically, they can in any case endeavor to become better.

To advance personal development in your teen, assist them with distinguishing their qualities just as their shortcomings. Then, at that point connect with them in objective setting and critical thinking so they can run after working on in regions where they battle. Ensure the objectives they set are to achieve that goal.

Recognition Exertion Rather than Result

Maybe than acclaim your teen for getting a passing mark on a test, acclaim them for all the examining they did. Rather than saying, "Incredible occupation scoring those five focuses in the game," say, "All that rehearsing you've been doing has been paying off." Show them that make a decent attempt and it's alright on the off chance that they don't succeed all the time.

Your teen can handle their work however they can't generally control the result. Recognize their energy and exertion so they don't think they are just deserving of acclaim when they succeed.

Show assertiveness Abilities

Teens need to realize how to support themselves in a proper manner. A decisive teen will actually want to request help when they don't comprehend school work, instead of permit themselves to fall behind.

A teen who can shout out likewise is less inclined to be dealt with inadequately by peers. They'll support themselves when they don't care for how they're being dealt with, and they'll have the option to request what they need in an immediate way.

To train your teen to be self-assured, start by discussing the contrast between being decisive and being forceful. Tell them that being decisive means supporting themselves utilizing a solid and sure voice without being inconsiderate or shouting at others.

CHAPTER SIX

WAYS TO IMPART ASSERTIVENESS SKILLS

Permitting them to settle on decisions and supporting that they have rights—particularly the option to deny anything that makes them awkward. Offer them adequate chances to rehearse their assertiveness abilities at home by offering them decisions and permitting them the opportunity to deny things they would prefer not to do.

BENEFIT FROM LEARNING TO BE ASSERTIVE

Encourage new opportunities

Attempting new exercises, finding covered up abilities, and testing themselves can assist with developing youngsters' certainty. Yet, numerous adolescents fear disappointment and don't have any desire to humiliate themselves.

Urge your teen boy to join another club, play an instrument, participate in charitable effort, or figure out low maintenance work. Dominating new abilities will help them rest easy thinking about themselves. In addition, having a place with a gathering furnishes them with fellowship openings, yet it additionally can help them have a sense of safety and sure.

Model Confidence

Your teen boy will become familiar with the most about certainty dependent on what you do—not what you say. In case you're blameworthy of offering basic expressions about your body or your capacities, you'll help your boy to do likewise.

Good example how to confront new circumstances with mental fortitude and certainty and show the significance of adoring yourself. Converse with your boy about occasions when you've been fearless or things you've done in your life to assist with building your certainty.

Build self-worth

On the off chance that your teen boy possibly feels great when they get a specific measure of preferences via online media or when they fit into a specific size pants, they'll battle to keep up with certainty when circumstances don't exactly measure up for their requirements. Putting together self-esteem with respect to shallow things, outer conditions, or others prompts an absence of trust over the long run.

Help your teenager form a sound and stable establishment for self-esteem. Underline your qualities and instruct that genuine self-esteem is tied in with living as indicated by those qualities. Help them see that be thoughtful and caring as opposed to thin or attractive.

Balance freedom with guidance

Micromanaging your teen's decisions will just support that they can't be trusted to use sound judgment autonomously. Equilibrium the perfect measure of opportunity with a lot of direction.

Give your teen a lot of freedoms to rehearse the abilities you've educated. Allow them to encounter normal outcomes and they'll gain from their own slip-ups. Over the long run, they'll foster expanded trust in their capacity to settle on solid decisions.

Normal Results as a Successful Discipline Apparatus

Assist with creating Positive Self-Talk

Your teen's inward talk will assume a significant part by the way they feel about themselves. In case they are continually thinking things like, "I'm so terrible," or "Nobody likes me," they will undoubtedly feel awful about themselves. Help your boy to foster solid self-talk.

Point out the number of contemplations aren't correct and help them perceive how being excessively brutal can be negative. Instruct them to rethink unreasonable contemplations like, "I will fall flat since I'm dumb," with something more sensible like, "I can pass math class on the off chance that I buckle down."

A Word of Advice

At the point when a teen has certainty, they can face challenges, break new ground, and go for the things they need throughout everyday life. Having certainty might even add to their strength particularly in case they are furnished with the thought that they will recuperate from even the most troublesome difficulties.

To help your teen's confidence, make certainty constructing a normal piece of your nurturing. Reliably challenge them, urge them to attempt new things, and above all to trust in themselves in any event, when they fall flat. Help them put forward objectives and afterward be their greatest team promoter zeroing in more on their diligent effort instead of the genuine outcomes. With exertion and consistency, you will construct a trust in your adolescent that will help them climate even the most troublesome misfortunes.

On the off chance that you notice that despite your endeavors your youngster actually battles with uneasiness or is showing indications of sorrow, converse with your primary care physician about your interests. It's conceivable that their low confidence is the aftereffect of a psychological well-being issue. With appropriate treatment and care, they can handle this test and figure out how to be surer about the cycle.

Printed in Great Britain
by Amazon